CSU Poetry Series XXIII

Veronica Patterson
5/29/90

Veronica Patterson

How to
Make a Terrarium

Cleveland State University Poetry Center

ACKNOWLEDGMENTS

Grateful acknowledgment is made to the publications below, in which some of these poems first appeared.
BUCKLE: "Tea"
THE CAPE ROCK: "The Dream" (from "The Knife Drawer")
COLORADO-NORTH REVIEW: "The Night Pasture," "On the Hatband Next to Size and Manufacturer"
COLORADO REVIEW (formerly COLORADO STATE REVIEW): "Ayre Street," "Grace"
CONCERNING POETRY: "The Woman Who Came Back From the Dead"
CROTON REVIEW: "How to Make a Terrarium," "Exquisite Manifold Ruler"
CUMBERLAND POETRY REVIEW: "Every Spring on Certain Nights"
DESCANT: "A Little Town Called Morrow," "The Necessary Unicorn"
ELEVEN: "Brooding"
GLENS FALLS REVIEW: "My Other Life"
INDIANA REVIEW: "Perspective"
KALLIOPE: "The Quests Arrive for Tea"
LOUISVILLE REVIEW: "Tweed Litany"
MADISON REVIEW: "The Past"
NEW LAUREL REVIEW: "The Skaters"
NEW MEXICO HUMANITIES REVIEW: "The Irrevocable Inch"
PIEDMONT LITERARY REVIEW: "Peter Bones"
POETRY-NORTH REVIEW: "Family Dinner," "Publishing the Banns"
SOUTHERN POETRY REVIEW: "Apples of October"
SOU'WESTER: "August," "The Woman at the Dike"
SPOON RIVER QUARTERLY: "The Etymology of Yellow," "Salt Lick"
TAURUS: "The Dream Decoder"
WINEWOOD JOURNAL: "Blue Fairy Blues"

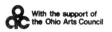

With the support of the Ohio Arts Council

CONTENTS

How to Make a Terrarium   7

"Always have wanted to live somewhere else"

The Year of the Inchworm   11
Brooding   12
The Secret Believer   13
Looking at Your Picture   14
The Hunters   15
Every Spring on Certain Nights   16
The Night Pasture   17
August   18
The Knife Drawer   19

**"Begin with gravel for drainage,
charcoal against souring."**

The Skaters   25
Ayre Street   26
Tweed Litany   28
My Life of Crime   29
Family Dinner   30
Peter Bones   32
At the Home   33
The Past   35

"Remember magic circles of string and chalk"

Tea   39
Publishing the Banns   41
On the Hatband Next to Size and Manufacturer   43
The Dream Man by the Jade Tree   44
Perspective   45
The Irrevocable Inch   46
A Little Town Called Morrow   47
The Necessary Unicorn   49

"a pine cone full of seeds"

In the Shape of a Child   53
Enter the Days   54
The Dream Decoder   55

The Woman Who Came Back from the Dead   56
Grace   57

"a pine seedling escapes"

My Other Life   61
Alone at Last   62
The Etymology of Yellow   63
The Woman at the Dike   64
The Dream of the Basket Babies   65
My Leper   66

"the wind blows through it"

In Which I Dream of Saving You   69
Firewatch   70
Blue Fairy Blues   71
Forget Me Not Blues   72
Elephant Leaves This Jungle   73
Exquisite Manifold Ruler   74
The Dream of the Jewel-Eyed Women   77

"needles ping faintly on broken glass"

The Annunciation   81
One of These Days   83
Provisioning God   84
Things I Never Did   85
The Quests Arrive For Tea   86
The One That Got Away   87
Remember the Mortar   89
Salt Lick   90
Apples of October   91

How to Make a Terrarium

HOW TO MAKE A TERRARIUM

Be a self-contained person.
Have just read *Sister Carrie*.
Always have wanted to live somewhere else.
Any transparent, waterproof container will do.
Remember Alice shrinking to a world
where one could drown in tears.
Begin with gravel for drainage,
charcoal against souring.
Be in a dry spell.
Use moss that springs back greener to the touch.
Wonder where the next words will come from.
Mix topsoil, sand, and leafmold.
Remember magic circles of string and chalk.
Form your own valleys, hills, cliffs.
"Arrange a world as you would have it."
Place in indirect light.
For color add partridge berries,
lichened rock, by accident,
a pine cone full of seeds.
Cover your terrarium with glass.
It will be cool, moist, make its own rain.
You must keep the soil lean lest
plants outgrow the container but

a pine seedling escapes
years later
the wind blows through it

needles ping faintly on broken glass

"Always have wanted to live somewhere else."

THE YEAR OF THE INCHWORM

The year we lived on Fall Creek Drive
where a vine-covered lattice
roofed the carport beneath my window
was the year of the inchworms.
All spring they hung pale on invisible threads
in the trees' budding gloom.
They caught on our clothes; one on my collar
made me tear off and stamp, shaking, on my jacket.
That year I had an English friend
who spoke oddly but helped me fill old beer bottles
with the worms: 77 in one seething bottle
died. He wore sweaters with leather buttons
and said America was amazing — all those worms.
On the piano the landlady taught me
"Chopsticks" on white keys and
"Peter, Peter, Pumpkin Eater" on black.
When shouting cramped the house, I saw myself
in embroidered silk kimono quietly bowing
in the concert halls of foreign cities.
In June a young man jumped from the suspension bridge.
The water ran loudly down the gorge as we watched
from above treetops, then crept down
the cool, muddy path
where everything was fern green and falling
and saw that the only movement
was water tugging his shirt.
They said that inchworms crossing the body
measured for new clothes
but I didn't grow
that spring.

Jung

"I had the overwhelming impression of having just emerged from a dense cloud. I knew at once: now I am myself!"

BROODING

she hovered and heckled me
from my damp curl in the arms
of the deep green chair,
suspecting me of hatching in silence
bloody stumbling
little creatures
that would grow

but mother, brooding dumb
in the web-rooted earth,
that's how things are born:

yolk of me white of you
egg of us brooded now
breaking

Freud

" . . . it is not only quite possible, but highly probable, that the dreamer really does know the meaning of his dream; *only he does not know that he knows.*"

THE SECRET BELIEVER

Your furious words pursued me
when I left to buy clothes for college,
"You belong in an asylum!"
I shrugged; accusations were not new.
But I had been to State at Christmas
and sung "Joy to the World" to bodies
half-covered in bleached and common cotton,
slumped and tied into chairs,
to mouths hanging open, uh-uh-uh,
repeating the sounding joy,
to twitching white limbs
and muffled shrieks down the halls.
For frankincense,
the sharp odor of urine.

And though I drove to the stores
and hung clothes on my body
and looked at myself in their windows,
an insistent voice warned,
"Impostor, play it safe.
Keep your mouth shut, reason clearly,
speak in no tongues nor to yourself.
Forget all dreams, even the field
of striped lilies."

For the secret believer knew
how the body raged
and the mouth drooled dreams
and cries muted with fists
were finished in pillows.

LOOKING AT YOUR PICTURE

for my sister

Remember the day of the winery
when we went with the photographer
to be the human measure?
In the stone building's shadow we shivered
as the keeper talked of vines
and bearing, chablis and burgundy,
chance, grafting, and heritage,
searching your light and my darkness
for common stock. When we smiled alike,
his face smoothed.
We stole through fermenting cellars
where sparkling wines lay cool on their sides
through vaults pungent with pressure and change
to where clarity poured from sediment.
Photographed by carved oak casks, at the foot
of metal tanks, we emerged to the slap of day,
stung by the rotting pulp and skins.
The old man said that even the angle of sun
on a certain turn of slope
could determine a wine's flavor.
Knowing the clouded house we returned to,
we moved closer, you squinting into the sun
as you do in this picture
I keep of my smile.

THE HUNTERS

Into our country house
isolated
in the fat brown interval
between the ready sweet potatoes
and the done turkey
three strangers came unshaven,
redfaced, stumbling,
set their guns against the wall
and sat next to them.
They swore they would share our dinner
and they did
though we ate on the Syracuse china.
Shrinking, my mother served
what my father carved
intent on his task
and we broke bread together, heads bowed
in the fumes of pocket whiskey.
So far, we learned,
they hadn't shot anything.
They fingered their guns,
grinning as we flinched to each click.
I prayed and chewed
and chewed and tried to swallow
that day of Thanksgiving,
that new world
still in my throat.

EVERY SPRING ON CERTAIN NIGHTS

every spring on certain nights
when the moon shone persistently
on her ritual lifting of spirits
my mother took to the road
wheels on gravel, the motor dimmed
in the distance my father sat
down to his reading
we watched each other with orphan eyes
asking nothing

once she took me with her
she drove mid-road, watched for nothing,
not the shocking statues of deer, wolfing farm dogs
all night we careened down twisting roads
above the glittering finger of lake

somewhere I jettisoned my fear
of police, being lost,
accident, death, her,
released the door handle, swayed
to each curve, drank the road
signs of counties we surveyed
the close trees, shut lilies, pale Queen Anne's lace
we trailed, riding night, sucking life
from the quiet breathing of cows, unlit farm houses,
rustling ditch weeds
and the rocking road and the wind of us
until the dark, sure figure beside me turned
between the still wagonwheels of the driveway

now each high-mooned spring night
I stand at the window and see my face
with the moon through it and don't drive
along roads muffled in trees
down whispering ditches;
I have my own ways of leaving
and returning, my own orbit

THE NIGHT PASTURE

Spreading old army blankets
among cows dimly visible,
we ate our secret candy,
bared our hot skin
until the breeze carrying
the thick odor of clover
thinned and cooled, and we wished
to press our nakedness
against the warm holstein hides
of Lucy and Princess.
All night, bulky shadows loomed
and retreated.
We almost dreamed of Crown, the bull,
who had paced his pen all day
in blistering sun,
but covered ourselves
with the prickling wool,
listened to all the stirrings
as heat lightning
flawed the edge of night.

AUGUST

The summer my father went abroad
and sent back exotic perfumes
mother took each province of France
she could not see
out of my skin.
True, the car broke down
and the well-pump was fused by lightning,
but worse, I had a job
and a boy.
He came that August, the sound of his car
heard miles away, carried
through heatwaves at sundown
to my eager ears.
How she hated my pleasure, my boy,
my escape. She drank and drank to it, then,
"Slut!" she screamed as I left,
"I know where you're going."
I went to Syracuse and Elmira
and the hills above the lake
where nothing happened.
Oddly, it was despair
that kept me from trouble.
I couldn't tell him, nor her, nor anyone,
how stars swung low to rake open my body,
tiger lilies in ditches whispered fierce reproaches,
every path led to flattened grass
where a chase ended in death or coupling,
in either case, blood.
I wish I could have said to her,
don't shout, don't shout,
hold me.
I'm dying as fast as you'd wish.

THE KNIFE DRAWER

1. *The Reality*

In the drawer,
the carving knife, bone handle
rutted deeper than peach stone lies
like words screamed.

●

Who told this relative
stranger which blade to hone
or rasped it over
the stained sharpener
never nailed to a wall
so we could move away?

●

You can go home
again, you cannot not
reset old places,
repeat lines no matter
who's at table until
one time the blood
runs clear,
the knife strikes bone,
rings out release —

then on the crystal knife rest
awaits the next roast bound
for the family platter.

2. *The Truth*

Who starts the music? Who first
dons tights and spangles, stands
at board inviting knives

to shape the body true
to life?

A knife thrower needs
a second who believes
no thrill
without blood, a stake
in the heart and

loves the knife,
fingers its blunt handle.
When he dies
it will be hers
to sharpen,
keep in a drawer, use
on family
occasions.

3. *The Dream*

Over and over he carves
rare roasts
but under the table
deals knives he sharpens
whetstone nights.

They thud next to her ear
cut hair that falls
in wings smooth as
slices for a sandwich.

The knives outline in black
where the body lies.
He guesses white flesh

of the breast, soft thighs well done,
guesses but will not know.

When the music stops,
there are none between her legs
where she bleeds anyway,
none in the heart.
In tights, dull spangled shirt
he stands
bone knife in hand:

he may want her to live.
It is with that
twisting in flesh
that she awakens.

4. *The Poem*

We loved dark woods
carried knives
in leather sheaths
on our belts.

Too soon I fired my blade,
forged a chain for my neck,
cut the sheath into bookmarks
for mysteries with solutions,
used only table knives
though they rang warnings
on bone china.

Each double-edged link
cut neck insisting
things be what they are.

●

I build a fire
hammer link with link, chanting

dagger   sword   poniard
scimitar   saber   rapier

a cutler's daughter needs
two blades:
one to cut white webs of gristle
to bone, saw through
to marrow,
two to dance.

"Begin with gravel for drainage,
charcoal against souring."

THE SKATERS

it begins like this:
you go skating at dusk
when bluing stains the snow
there is a moon; if your mother were here
she would call you in
streetlights come on, hurl shadows iceward
at your left elbow he appears
you know him
he is the one your mother warned of
gently he grips your elbow, smoothly
glides; you waltz no daylight dance until
you see his face: black hair,
white scar, teeth like tiger stripes
eyes
you lean away from; his arm
defines your will

downriver, you skate toward spring and falls
of distant thunder; the ice bubbles but
still you skate
over your mother's face;
she screams at the slash but
not at you
she wants him back, wants to cut him again with nails
he turned and drove through her own palms;
a bruised hand breaks from the ice to clutch his blade

she knew him well
the man in the car with candy
the man in the bushes at the park
the one in the black jacket
with the black jack
of spades
in the corner, nimble, quick
of the bean
stalking
and I never saw him before in all her life

AYRE STREET

When shadows stained the day
and games dissolved over lawns,
we knew it was time.
You turned the corner,
red hair floating in sun,
and we ran, heedless
of sunken squares,
down the long sidewalk.
There was time to believe
as our canvas sneakers pounded
and lifted again, that crimes and wounds
would be forgotten or healed,
the day absolved of undertow.
To think, as we sailed the wind
we made, that though we were hungry,
there would be dinner
and perhaps nickels for the ice cream man
before night drowned the grass.

Though we knew the evening would shut down
to the light over one table
where you sat,
the hushed border we wore around you,
the shifting, tidal darkness.

Still, there was time to hope,
your face looming larger and larger,
just before our bodies, swollen with need,
thudded against you,

that tonight would be different.
That we would not fall asleep
submerged in longing

for what we couldn't name
but must have,
that we believed
running down the street faster every night

you would give us.

TWEED LITANY

a good tweed   coat of bitterness
my mother said   coat of hooks
will never wear out   coat of iron
terrified at fifteen   coat of dismay
given the coat   coat of dull
blue white brown   coat of no apples
that didn't fit   coat of her life
anything more recent   coat of ancient history
than grandmother's Roman times   coat of lions
though I discarded it   coat of acid
when possible   coat of discontent
ugly and warm   coat of arms
when she wasn't   coat of anger
yet I would hear again   coat of confession
her words   coat of loss
I'd wind to myself   coat of spinning

gone now to the Isle of Skye   coat of too far
coat   mother   coat of no return
mother   coat of yearning
into the chill   coat of tissue thin
draft she never countered   coat of scarves
where lost objects   coat of wishes
may be found again   coat of the longest odds
may find each other   coat of us
I see her now   coat of black watch
in my coat of few colors   sky, earth, paper
as I shiver in this   coat of words

MY LIFE OF CRIME

I don't know why I took them,
the red-and-silver wrapped peppermints,
because I wanted
the moon. Round and mottled,
perhaps they reminded me of it
or of Christmas
that never brought enough
of Christ or presents.
I remember the bright drug store,
my father afterward, shame,
but mostly confusion.
How I couldn't say, what I want is
to be a concert pianist
but there's no money for lessons,
to be a ballerina
but I have no toeshoes,
to be my father's daughter.

If they had only understood
how stupid the candy was, a mistake,
but not the kind they thought.
An escape valve of desire
steaming briefly into cold air
that January I had no boots.

FAMILY DINNER

The faces link
around the table.
The dark ripe olives
yield their hard secrets
and each linen napkin
unfolds its story
while the silver chatters louder
than the river over stones.

On the porch
shaded by old pines
the scalloped corn beds snugly
in eggs and cream,
green beans snap to attention,
measured like children
against other years,
and the roast waits,
bound and bleeding,
while yellowed recipes —
imprecise as the stories —
pass hand to hand.

Black coffee cools to grounds
the sun leaves to scale
east canyon wall.

Too soon, beside each fork,
deep dish peach pie,
thick and warm, on which
ice cream melts
faster than the faces
in summer heat.

Next summer
at the cabin
where the road forks

we will drink
from the river in spoons
and remember the faces
like knives.

PETER BONES

though bone refuses flesh
Judas time has kissed her with
tomorrow
(and drops of rain run silver
down the window)
brittle bone refuses flesh
finding dry geometry
a thinner cleaner life

holding pain
like a wafer on her tongue
she chews and
in wine of saliva
though bone refuses flesh
swallows
this unleavened afternoon

AT THE HOME

1. What shall I say
when I've taken your hand in the hall?

that the children have the flu
but will visit soon?

that geese stay the winter
and chase the cat from the yard?

that in your room the red amaryllis
burns the yellow curtains?

2. I rub your aching legs.
You ask the time, the day.
We stumble on who's and when's
repeating "what?"

I tell the weather like a story:
how clouds formed on the mountains,
rose on slate, and flooded the sky,

late sun dropped in ladders
without angels and the temperature
dropped to zero.

3. It is always warm here
but you are cold. I find a blanket
for your lap.

In the face of pain, words swirl away
like black birds from corn stubble,
flying south.

I hold your hand,
not reading the palm,

and come back to the weather
that also can't be changed
but doesn't hurt:
snowpack, chinook, melting that's to come.

THE PAST

do you remember those thick nights
deep in the country
our heavy Plymouth Dad said
steered like a boat?
on a hill we disengaged the clutch
left the car in neutral and coasted
slick and fast down the winding road
to the still, deep lake
wondering would it float

"Remember magic circles of string and chalk."

TEA

Under certain circumstances, there are few hours in life more
agreeable than the hour dedicated to the ceremony known as
afternoon tea.

— Henry James, *Portrait of a Lady*

If, with rainwater
I steep you fragrant tea
of lemon grass and thistle,
would you sip it steaming
and brew honeysuckle
and soursop to full body

for me to swallow
as we measure
twisted leaves of horehound
and in aromatic nights
gather wild holly

afterward dipping into
jars of our eyes
for bitter tally and sage

if, when we toss dry orchids
and jasmine into
a common bowl
they bloom to full size
with gardenias like
ears really listening, and

if, on our knees at last,
we drink our amber infusion
to old porcelain and
rough pottery, still
which of us would dare
to tell our fortune
in smoky black

if, to your lavender,
I still say cochineal
to your lovage, clove
to your linden, lime
could we go on

carrying our breakable bowl
and separate cups, brewing
from unlabelled jars
a pungent blend?

PUBLISHING THE BANNS

A band on one curved finger,
softly she plucks steel strings
(like thread and needle)
a tune
he was pleased to dance to.

At night she turns
and turns
morning finds her
wound and warm,
him cold.

Her spool played out in
hemming party gowns —
she sees
the end, wants
the thread back.

As she winds,
bands tighten round him —
tourniquets for wounds
she makes
that never loosen

until each extremity
can be removed
with little pain or blood.
He doesn't miss but one.
As she cares for him
in white
he sees he needs her.

Spool turning, she re-coils
bandages for future wars
knit from threads
unstitched from clothes

he doesn't need
that fall in patterned pieces
and unravel.

Mannequin shivers.
She twines him maypole fancy
round and round
with strands she'll have
back soon. They are silk,
they shimmer and wrap
at first like warmth.
But this is not a cocoon:

nothing will be born
but a worm that
circles the mulberry bush
spinning black silk for
inked ribbons
that won't reverse —

leaving one spool empty,
one full: neither moves.
Words grow lighter;
no message is left
stitched on
the winding sheet.

ON THE HATBAND
NEXT TO SIZE AND MANUFACTURER

I would like to have it noted that
when the eleventh hour came
and we knew it

we volunteered together
climbed the steps and

(ignoring the audience
the heat of the lights
the dark magician)

reached the clasped bare hands
we'd always held
into the black silk hat

and pulled out
a complacent white rabbit
we placed gently on the stage and

during the applause
while the magician bowed
climbed in

THE DREAM MAN BY THE JADE TREE

admires it as
I turn pale green and silent
breaks a branch porcelained
with years saying
he'd never seen one fuller
crouches by the pot
face turned from me
bumping thick-leaved branches saying
he'd never seen one rounder
fingers each polished leaf he plucks
deliberately flattens each curve and
mounded in succulent tears he loves
my jade plant so
it may not live

PERSPECTIVE

A charcoal night.
The painted woman drives home yellow
lights blink before and behind her past
bedtime past the hospital where
the ambulance howls pain
drowning regrets of her red need
for an affair of the
palette. She has been to her color man
who dances, tells her stories, lies, seeds
sticky tar babies she must raise
like questions
and they paint the town primarily
in shadow. Tomorrow she'll pay for every hue
and cry.

Tonight, when she reaches home, the other waits
in the dark room. One pale foot flung
over her half of the bed
highlights her green return.
Webbed blue veins texture
the skin impasto of strings or
rivers one could follow.

She brushes his foot.
It withdraws, unlike a
Venus trap, asking little, perhaps
not her rainbow life. Freed,
she hears his breathing deepen.
She makes a frame of her fingers;
how she sees this
matters.

THE IRREVOCABLE INCH

inch by inch we go our separate ways
and geometry demands
that no matter how small the angle,
just one degree, the first in burns,
can start a fire that chars night,
sears morning, leaves a no man's land
of blackened stumps

inch by inch we go our separate ways
and even if lines parallel
they may be held by rigid, tarry ties —
a photograph album, a child's elastic shadow;
at midnight, a train-child cries, wakes me
to watch your eyes quicken
under feather lids we never lift;
the train hurries into dark
having come, somehow, between us

inch by inch we go,
walking sticks forked like tongues
we rub for warmth,
wishbones we must loosen in our hands
divine or drown of thirst

give me your hand
come watch the meteor showers
we have time for
nothing
else
and our bodies crave the moisture

though the meteors don't fall far
between our fingers,
they don't come back an inch

A LITTLE TOWN CALLED MORROW

1. what was it that you wore
when we met
was it becoming?
and was your favorite riddle
the one about a stream
with animals to be crossed
but of any pair in the boat
one would eat the other?

2. I used to be able to
name your tune, in fact
knew all the bass doo-ahs;
when you forgot the words
I sang them back, now
the only music I hear
is marching to the buzzer
to pass the question on

3. do you remember when
I dressed you in suits? diamonds,
hearts, spades — you patient in the
trumpery of prince, priest, pirate
I was certain you wanted to be something
else

4. other times I take things
too personally; one week I thought
you used up all the underwear
in your drawer *on purpose*

5. were you to be Orpheus
and I Eurydice
and one of us looked back?
or was it beauty and the beast,
the sleeping beast?

6. our three worst arguments were over
how to make a friend
whether the game of Hearts is like Old Maid and
how we argue

7. divorce has subtle forms I knew a man
who left while there, a woman
who killed herself alive

8. together we dream solitary dreams
but apart
share a torn nightmare with edges
that heal a parchment map of rivers

9. we have no words for what we are
and it's a matter of rendering:
if glue can be made of
skin, bone, hooves

10. it may seal this letter
ticket enclosed
if it reaches you in time
meet me at the end
of this line

THE NECESSARY UNICORN

In this world, the woman's head is bent as a sunflower;
some day the children will roast or plant her eyes.
Her mouth is underground, but her eyes cry out through
goldenrod where butterflies are windows.

In this world, the man is a wicker trap full of fish, time
the curious cat with probing eyes.

The child's face is made of violets; eyes rise on stalks from roots
that spread each year. Purple breathes into the night.

A woman stands naked before the moon; thick vines twine up her legs
but her head is in clouds or she has no head or
the moon is her head.

Why does he dress in a dark suit, hold an umbrella over the yellow pear
in high heels? He will eat her ripe face and leave the core.

The barred door of a child's head opens; there are tiger's eyes in dark
and pearls already free; the child thinks the open shells can fly.

Why should the eyes marry a dancing bear in a suit? Why does the bride
have no legs but shoes? Because the organ grinds.

In the eyes of the necessary unicorn, lean wolves on a snowy ridge
fade in the garden lap of his dreams; he must awaken, be still, imagine
their hot loins from inside; survive.

The black butterflies assault her, beat on bare breasts; embraced by the largest,
already her hair parts and flies; in a cloud below the waist, damp
unfolding wings live some dark hours. This too is a dream.

The man is a honeycomb and she a wasp with delusions of nightshade purple
yet the orange berries crush, ferment, can be stored in waxy hexagons
with these sides:

1. the catfish with a third eye
2. shells that fly
3. the organ grinder's monkey
4. the unicorn that was never a narwhal
5. open-toed shoes full of seed
6. a readiness to move on

They leave.tomorrow;
everywhere they step
rue flowers
in the shape of their feet.

"a pine cone full of seeds"

IN THE SHAPE OF A CHILD

I sang my way to the birth
in quickening rhythm;
you danced in white with mask
for the new girl's coming.

From the first
they would not let me have her
but they swore
I could hold her soon.

Morning brought no child
to my room
but assurance —
she'd be there, soon.

Milk came in body time
and they whispered
soon, now, soon.

Then at night
she was "holding her own"
against what
they would tell me. Soon.

Too soon
you returned to sirens wailing,
wailing what I knew:
she'd been dying
since she was born.

And the body, dumb, slow
stubborn keeper of promises,
shaped a grief to the child:
broke sleep, rained milk, bent down,
cradled arms. Rocked.

ENTER THE DAYS

Brooding day and night
I guard your sleep
but everywhere cracks widen,
those of dawn
almost unbridgeable.

With frettings twisted
into nets of prayer,
arms flung in desperate fence,
jaws locked, breath stopped
to hush the waiting sirens —
with all I have —
I guard your sleep,
who dream of tightroping
this holding pattern.

It becomes more difficult
to still each limb,
to keep the stiff sheet
on your stirring body,
the pillow under your head:
to lull your waking.

Arched above the nest
to shield your eyes
my body dries
to silence.

I guard your sleep
on this the sixth day.
The nest floats.
You close unclouded eyes.

THE DREAM DECODER

Last night I almost had it.
When I arrived at the church
the young man was entering figures in a ledger.
He began the decoding session.
First, he said, do not number the pages.
Below the table, I numbered mother's stack
of grocery receipts. Out of order, I might miss
her message, and it was all she'd left.
Each page, he said, contains three numbers
arranged like this: a three in the upper left corner,
twenty-four a third down the page on the right,
and seven at center bottom.
I looked at mine: zucchini, golden apple,
tax, total, check, change,
thinking of cereal eaten
for a magic decoder ring.
His words didn't seem to apply.
We moved to pews.
The scripture was Christ's question:
is there no message for me.
The text was the value of silence
versus words
when there's nothing to tell.
As he began, I felt water splashed from behind
in the darkened church. I kept the receipts
dry. Stale, they tasted faintly of sweat.

I woke damp,
my daughter by the bed
watching. I have nothing to tell her
yet.

THE WOMAN WHO CAME BACK FROM THE DEAD

As it turns out
they were not finished with her yet.
She could hear their voices faintly through the glass
but kept her eyes shut.
She had feared this; glass between them,
no touch.
Her skin stretched again to meet them.
They could not see that beneath the coffin she held
a baby with dark hair
that would never change
her mother's hand for the first time
grandmother guided the dead line.
They had danced.

But they lifted the glass and despite
the coldness kissed her despite the skin that clung
to their green fruit hands, they
took hers.
Could they make love again out of
these things: voices, fear of glass, hands, and
a song she remembered? It didn't seem much to go on.
But the flesh she had lost seemed
not to be essential; she would be needing
less from now on.
The bones that showed were not the polished white
she had expected but opalescent
as a sunfish she had caught once
and kept alive in a pail for quite some time,
as neons who lived with her guppies,
as the nickelodeon in which the children put
all their allowance:
put another nickel in
in the nickelodeon
all I want is loving you
and music, music,
music.

GRACE

for my daughters

I enter your room at night
and walk to your bed
as to a table,
thirsty for the milk
of your skin,
the smooth bubble
of lid over eye.
Your hair spreads a cornucopia
around your heated cheeks,
the rare pink slice
of your lips,
the risen curve of forehead.
Your fingers lie on the blanket
white as asparagus raised in the dark.
You stir, and I move
back. Do not awaken.
You would think me
some haunting overseas waif
from a page of *Time*
whose swollen belly
bore a hunger
I gave your name to.
Perhaps I should stay
a little less long each night
toward the day you leave,
but I have no will.
Gently I tuck the sheet
close beneath your chin.
Sleep, sleep,
until I have my fill.

"a pine seedling escapes"

MY OTHER LIFE

in my other life
I write more poems
do not give birthdays for children
who eat my life in wedges
of cake to be baked, rooms cleaned
and decorated in yellow crepe streamers
but each year travel to foreign countries
meditate in the ornate shadows of churches
bring back, if not home, curiosities
in brass, fragments of authentic tapestries
I speak of aesthetic surfaces and clouds
of unknowing, not today and tomorrow
revel in shades of meaning
have intricate affairs — ecstatic nights and rules,
long letters and declines —
I read deep and late, sleep when I wish
my room stays clean
in my other life
I sit at a polished desk by a high window
without a daily man
not thinking of a party loud with horns
ballooning to red burst unwrapped
from surprise balls —
of being used —
but in my other life
I don't dare write this down

"The first achievement of the dream work is condensation . . . the manifest dream is less rich than the latent thought."

Freud

ALONE AT LAST

I arrived at the hospital alone at dusk.
(I am always alone at dusk).
A magnolia tree by the curved drive was
burning its pale candles for all it was worth.
I opened double brass doors to a table where nurses
and orderlies, faces looming yellow in the thick smoke,
bent over a poker game.
They resented my arrival.
They could not find my admission slip in the file.
At last one impatient nurse found my name filed under
The Ambassadors; this was their "favorite novel" filing system.
I protested that was not my favorite novel
but saw myself from their point of view
and dropped the matter.
In a hospital gown in a bedless room I waited.
You came at seven, just before full dark.
You carried me around on your shoulders
and we laughed. We danced, I in my gown, we remembered,
we remembered. Then you said, "This is the time for
bending down." You set me on the floor.
You had to leave.
You left.
The insuck of my breath dried the cry in my throat.
I couldn't leave now. I couldn't remember
what the operation was or why it was necessary:
cut away from you like this
flesh from bone,
sinews white and broken,
the world seeming just one bead cut loose
from my string
leading to God
knows where.

THE ETYMOLOGY OF YELLOW
in the pack of color cards, yellow is life

gold easily scratched
butter melted
ripe lemon
of the dress my mother wore
a dark belt slashed
juice ran
burning in wounds
staining the dress
curling the yellowed picture

the roots lie deep
in fields of mustard
where I hid like a seed
beneath curved stems

October holds out yellow
against November, holds out
razor-petaled chrysanthemums
she planted by the house:
they hurt my eyes

there were warning signs
on the road to the white house
I painted yellow the walls
of the rooms I lived in
wearing yellow gloves winter long

knowing blades grew
that would fall
to spill this yellow,
free this wet, thin-boned
bird who stumbles, hungry
at the line

between the color and the fear of the color

THE WOMAN AT THE DIKE

from the dike she cannot see
the fields behind her
for it takes the fingers of both hands
stretched wide
to fill the holes

she cannot see
deer browse at dusk,
leaves turning pale
to spot the fawns of spring

she only sees the wall,
her desperate fingers,
and water rising in green tons
against her

at night, exhausted,
she leans against cold clay,
dreaming there is no water,
that she could move her fingers

she yearns to make a fist,
pick daffodils,
play wet stops
on a piccolo of water

imagining through the holes
a tulip country
where windmills whirl
to stir delft skies

or these might be handholds
with more above her;
she can't tell from here

she can't ever tell from here

THE DREAM OF THE BASKET BABIES

That shape am I.

— William James

Inside the operating room
the x-ray machine's head began to snake after me:
I kept out of reach, as usual.
A doctor arrived with his middle-aged wife.
She carried a basket she gave to me.
A plump, blond baby
blinked its slow blue eyes.
I lifted it from the basket; it began to walk.
The basket wasn't empty.
Another baby, thin and dark, brown eyes quick
with pain, lay there flattened. The face was torn,
as if something pushed from within.
I cradled it in my arms.
It was limp, its breathing too loud.
In the basket still was a black terrycloth man
with shoebutton eyes.

The doctor and his wife left
me holding the baby, the blond child
stumping merrily around the room, lonely
as Goliath. Reflected in a moving eye
I made a pillow of the cloth man,
laid the dark baby's head there gently
rubbing brown limbs. Then, mouth to mouth,
I began.

MY LEPER

I kick my leg above my head
see, I say, see
but my leper
does it with no foot
and everyone applauds

I tie intricate knots,
build a string cathedral
see, I say, see
with stump of wrist and teeth
my leper strings a harp
that calls each in to pray

I paint my body orange and black
to tell my tiger stories
listen, I say, listen
my leper does not hide her sores
beneath the moon they shine like pools
of fish like silver coins
enough to feed the poor

and the people weep for her
no matter what I do
how I perform
they turn
to my leper

"the wind blows through it"

IN WHICH I DREAM OF SAVING YOU

"Then there were crushings in the underbrush, and a gigantic wolfhound with a fearful, gaping
maw burst forth . . . It tore past me and I suddenly knew: the Wild Huntsman had commanded it
to carry away a human soul."

there was an old woman

> You sat at the table
> in a dim corner of the restaurant,
> dark beret at an angle, tweed skirt
> and tailored jacket just so:
> a member of the French resistance,
> bones lighting skin already
> made lamp.
> Two chairs were empty.

lived under a hill

> An old woman, torn black coat
> around swollen ankles,
> sat down, shoulders hunched
> beneath pale scalp punctured
> thinly by hair.
> You looked at her with distaste.
> Toothless, she grimaced,
> her fingers plucking the top
> of a rumpled brown bag.

and if she's not gone

> I hurried to the table with my daughter.
> "These chairs have been saved for us," I insisted.
> Eyes watering, she looked at me, rose,
> shuffled off closing her bag.
> I glanced around;
> she had not gone far.

she lives there still

> She wants your shining bones.

69

FIREWATCH

Notes of an incipient pyromaniac

How lucky she was
he proposed nothing
that dry October day
when the radio warned of fire
and all the leaves were yellow.
She might have said yes
because he'd brought her
down the dirt road to this:
slender trunks, sun through leaves
like thin skin, saplings
blinding her eyes,
undergrowth melting her knees,
gilding even her feet
yellow
until she was dizzy with it.

Now, a half-life later,
such a day smolders long,
for she knows more
of consequences
but feels the parch of years.
And she knows someone,
a spinner of straw
into this combustible garment
she must shed
against the fall.

Wait,
do not touch her
in this yellow time
that smells of smoke
or else,
beloved else.

BLUE FAIRY BLUES

suppose you were born without it
and it was all you wanted

it's invisible; you pretend
for years you have it,
watching those who do,
mimicking,
knowing better

you discover what it's made of:
fighting the cancer of days,
crying ecstasy,
falling from cliffs of grace,
slowly mending,
making promises in the dark
to be kept
in the bodies of children

you find flesh is necessary:
though not flesh
it lives there
only

you end up like Pinocchio's father,
building it of wood and strings
thinking — *real* —
making it dance,
wrestling with despair
as it grows light and wide in truth,
shrinks, plummets
with each lie

you sit every night at the window

FORGET ME NOT BLUES

One day as I was walking down the
avenue I met a flower man walking his pet
snapdragon. He the man had ears
like gardenias and a face as open
as a four-o-clock (it was only two)
and a head that bent to me
like a sunflower, reverent
as hell and eyes more velvet than purple
violas you must touch to believe.
His hair was orange as poppies in
a California field after a wet spring
in 1967. In his hand
he held a daisy chain
he wanted me to wear,
for my neck, he said
the greenest things
as he promised chrysanthemums
like suns when it grows cold
and ever asters
and 10,882 other flowers
and he said he knew a place where
forget-me-knots bloomed early
but I asked about later, winter.
He said I asked too much
and though he had an iris tucked behind
each ear and a tiger lily in his teeth
and all kinds of roots and bulbs about him
and though I was drawn in his musky footsteps,
I said, a chain's a chain.
He stopped and shrugged and left
in a swirl of dandelion fluff
and he hasn't thought of me since, sure as
zinnias, nor
I of him.

ELEPHANT LEAVES THIS JUNGLE

you are numbered among the tigers
I have feared the saber teeth
gleaming in hours of dark truth,
the punishing claws I have felt
for sins of mistaken identity,
your leaping quickness, but know that
you lose more than a tiger's share, fear
the broad feet that balance on your quicksand roar,
envy the way I eat treetops you climb to,
my long gestation, and my memory:
in this flesh-bound trunk I keep my answers
with questions you never asked; they bed
symmetrical, arousing,
leading to no consummate final choice,
no triumphant O'Henry trick
for this short story, these years
of the tiger

leading only to a glimpse of the clearing
where we might have met
you fearing the tonnage
and I the incision
a prodigious stripping and leaving
not this dear distance

you are numbered among the tigers
whose eyes search and destroy nights;
am I among secret elephants
that drift through gray forests of sleep or smoke
down some artery or nerve you have
barred the world in which I wander
prisoner without stripes

EXQUISITE MANIFOLD RULER

It is a true debt it can never be paid.

— W.S. Merwin

when I made you my cartographer
I took your measurements
as you quartered the country of my mind
surveying meters I moved
from here to some Magellan there
of your plotting perhaps
just an isle of you
I had your number
of the millimeters I climbed
ratioed to the thickness of ties
that bound me
down

you roamed
the topography of my sins
detector of damp-palmed truths   pith-helmeted
ticking in thickest jungle to active deposits,
veins of ore, half-lives so far inland
and underground, assaying the necessary shaft,
my major miner how
you did dig

now you would not compass but send me
on straight lines a distance
you never measure
between us   ignoring curves
we throw each other, temperatures on any scale
my inclinations   in the far desert
you say I must cultivate
I will grow
Jerusalem artichokes and bitter herbs

overseer with your joy in gauging
I bequeathed you the calibrated eyeball

whose existence   I now see
my father maintained
to strip and weigh me before him
finding, leaving me
wanting
I thought never to grant his privilege

except to some gracious oceanographer
of extreme longitude adept
with quadrant and spirit level
sensor of rainfall's possible rivers
generating words like lighthouses —
a fathomer of bushels

not to you grand inquisitor of the last degree,
phrenologist of my heart,
private eye of my infidelities,
instrument of my incision,
engineer of burning ships and bridges,
geographer of courage,
bureau of the weights I drag,
scourge of my early deaths

earthmover, who needs
this constant quaking
of the ground beneath Richter feet?

jack   jack   maybe knave
or king of all
my weather-moving trade winds
free me of your everlasting
altimeter, the scales that weigh me
down

no

internal ruler now green
fecund inching grub of spring measuring tape

worm coiled feeding on my life
turning all I eat for flesh
into uncountable words

measure me   measure me
that I may measure
up

THE DREAM OF THE JEWEL-EYED WOMEN

He had painted portraits of them all
in parrot orange, steaming scarlet,
Rousseau green. Jungle orchids
bloomed in their hair.
Sly, dusky skins shone damply,
their eyes inset emerald, ruby, topaz.
Walking the gallery, she stopped
before her portrait.
The eyes were aquamarine and flat
sharp facets glittered.
The brass plate below was engraved,
"She would not let the morning
past her eyes."
He had taken a likeness so good
she mourned her loss. Tears fell.
They were real and
wet. Would they be daily?
Emptied, could she go, now that
she had seen
she was not the light
but could witness
morning trapped
behind her eyes.

"needles ping faintly on broken glass"

THE ANNUNCIATION
after Rossetti's painting

1

she crouches to the wall,
shoulders hunched, pale and suspicious
as the young angel holds out a sinuous lily
the pulsing irrevocable pain of birth
the agony of hope, departure, death
must she witness this son
no one will understand
the angel is confident his hair
shining   the muscled arms   bare   his hand
holds her like a spell
she will not look at his face
he cares nothing for her
thinking it an honor
he will not come again until the choir sings
but not for her

already her scalp prickles with radiance
she feels the faint stirring
sees the wet afterbirth quiver on straw

II

hot against this pillow
footsteps approach
sitting up I crouch to the wall
away from the man
not a man   wings and a light
why does he offer that lily
wax and green as my skin
with its insistent odor of death
what does   he wants
my body for his god to garden

why should I out of tearing pain
and blood bring a new life

in death into the world   I would have
instead his body   those muscled arms
erect back   hair like field wheat
but he holds the open blossom
I look not a him but at the ignorant she-lily
spreading
to the wedge of light
behind him
I would not feel
come

ONE OF THESE DAYS

One of these days
I'm going to re-address
all the mail to itself — "please backward"
for a change I'm going to thaw
all the food I've frozen against God
knows what eventuality and feed it
to sparrows I'm not going to change
my clothes but go
as I am, cutting carpet away from walls
for a bag I'll fill with paper and pencils
already sharpened and no excuses
to drive north until I run
out of gas and walk until I have to
stop there, beyond Reproach,
where a man left his wife
to pan for gold and found it
dust, which was what he needed
to know. Thereafter,
I'll come back.
And if they ask why I went I'll say
it's neither here nor there
but I had to find out.

PROVISIONING GOD

Hunted down in time
this is how God eats me:
from me, scalded, gutted free at last,
he carves thick steaks for broiling,
haunches to smoke.
He knows once come, I will keep.

The ends of flesh
he grinds for pungent sausage
herbed with long resistance,
packed in organs emptied by his breath.

Chopping, salting, pressing,
he recalls the struggle, the craving,
savors most my delicate tongue.

As he stirs blood pudding
spiced with Sundays
he renders the heart
to stew
the tang of God,

then scrapes clean my skin,
oils, pieces with tendons
taut with holding back
a cloth
to wipe his face
when he is done   with me

satisfied at last,
made finally into his image.

THINGS I NEVER DID

I never leaned, blond and twenty,
in a strapless black lace leotard
against a scarecrow in striped pajamas
in a half-harvested autumn field
and set my matching baseball cap
by just two fingers on the brim
at the same jaunty angle as his

now
I will never be twenty
but could exercise
never be blond
but could dye my hair
or

I could bring red hot berries
of mountain ash
into my burning house,
lie on the porch at night
craving this distance from the stars
a little longer

late
I will do
wholly redundant things
smiling upon God
in my cap

THE QUESTS ARRIVE FOR TEA

Due to a typographical error
quests arrived for tea.
I had sent no invitations but they claimed
to be my quests. There stood the Quest
for Perfectly Polished Brass and the Quest for the Poem
That Sings Like a French Horn
Played Expertly and the Quest for Untenable Positions
Worth Maintaining and the Quest for
mother.
There were inquests, bequests, not to mention
requests (quests that kept returning despite)
like the Quest for Purity.
Each wished a different kind of tea. The Quest
for the Final Healing of Ancient Hurts wanted
chamomile and the Quest for You required passion
flowers, hawthorn berries, and skullcap.
One took sugar without lemon and the next
vice versa with the third wanting cream and
acting British and deploring my lack of crumpets
and Prince of Wales tea steeped just so.
One was a connoisseur — the Quest for Blooming
Days Without Thought of Future Good — and sniffed
the tea's bouquet of jasmine and memories.
Nothing would satisfy them: they insisted on everything.
The Quest for Passionate Sorrow and Joy quarreled
with the Quest for Daily Life Lived with Some Grace
and, after words, left.
The Quest for the father in me was reluctant to go
but had nothing to say. Never has.
All thanked me for my hospitality but none knew why
they'd been brought together. As host and go-between —
ambassador — I could tell them little: just the story
of my life. The Quest for the Indefinable
Something Beyond the Moon stayed
to hear it, lingering until afternoon gilded
the windows and ripened
our faces. And then it grew dark.

THE ONE THAT GOT AWAY

I

Once a fish learned to read.
She was swimming the square
when beyond the glass she saw
odd black marks on white.
She stared until they seemed to speak.
Each day they were different.

She began by making connections.
Daily she imagined what had happened
from one set to the next.
The glass didn't seem so flat.
The sets grew thicker, the marks more elusive,
the gaps wider. Her mind leaped crime
to punishment, war to peace to war, pride
to the ground. Intricate patterns
were broken by astonishments.
Then her own stories floated free.
Days were not long enough and she loved shimmering nights
when the light was left on and her bright world
shone into the dark.

You think it unlikely?
This is how it happens.
You wonder what was her ink,
how she limbered her fins,
what characters she used,
if she wrote on shells:

what has to be done, will be.

II

She yearned beyond the glass
where stories were whole,
spending time where water ended,

gulping gills hard and tight:
whole days alone at the edge of air.

Then one night
while the others slept
she put one fin over the rim
spun her tail, and

REMEMBER THE MORTAR

We sat in the Colosseum, waiting for our play to begin.
Suddenly, a plane crashed through the opposite wall.
Perhaps World War III had begun, I thought, but the plane
had a propeller and the pilot a scarf. He saluted.
Chunks of wall went flying. One piece the size of a door
zoomed to within inches of the leading man's face.
It left cartoon motion lines in the air. He quickly
picked up a book with a red and yellow, black and green cover
and began to read to Katharine Hepburn:
"Once upon a time in far-off Australia . . . "
She settled against his shoulder for the duration.
Beside me, you sighed ruefully and asked,
"How long do you think this will be?"
"As long as his life," I answered,
"remember the mortar."

SALT LICK

in the distance of words
I roll *bird* from my tongue
grudging *d,*
my hands
on the double edge
of your shoulder bones

I utter *plums*
but they fade in sibilance,
fall from the trees,
rot sweet to their pits
overwhelmed by your ripening

I say *light*
savoring the *I*
because you slip
into the morning room —
brilliant, still —
until I sense your presence

but stumble over *rivers*
as the veins beneath your skin
flow away;
tongue *stones*
that do not help me speak

turn at last
to *salt,*
craving the taste
of this game I play
with my tongue
licking these saline things —
pale but breathing on their own —
into shapes like waves flung
out of the sea, caught
just before they break

APPLES OF OCTOBER

Comfort me with apples.

1. Outside the window, almost hidden in ivy,
the bitten apple a squirrel dropped
hurrying toward November. I open the window
to that core smell.

2. Once I rode through the tracery of weeds
in a lost orchard, trees crippled,
branches empty, apples broken
into the earth, trampled to vinegar
that with leather, the sweat of horses,
stirred
the sharp odor of October.

3. One morning in Illinois
we picked from trees burdened with apples
that dragged the branches
down to the still-wet grass:
our bushel for these red Niagaras.
What could we do then but visit the mill,
drink juice opaque with pulp.

4. And all afternoon I ached
as if the apples had made a wound
only your body could staunch
pressing through flesh
bone to bone in the night.

5. The child died, but — no —
the child died *and*
one day in October you came
with apples so large
I could just hold one in my stretched hand.
Against — no — *into*
the still hum of death

the apple did not whisper
yet

6. it was something of red
and flesh and juice,
of the soursweet balance of October
that shifts
to spill and press its apples
into the earth, my hands, a cloudy cider
I can't see through,
                    but smell,
                              drink.